CONTENTS

INTRODUCTION AND ACKNOWLEDGEMENTS

My childhood interest in tramways began in the final days of the London system, however during the tramless 1950s and 1960s, it was to Eastbourne that I turned for inspiration. Visits were made from my grandparents' house near Hailsham and the object of my quest lay at the eastern end of town by Princes Park where a narrow gauge electric tramway provided transport for visitors to the South Coast resort.

This world of the narrow gauge, miniature tramway combines the skills of the model-maker/engineer with the demands of the full size prototype. It is an area first fully explored by Claude Lane (1908-71), who was the driving force behind the Eastbourne operation and the subsequent successful move to Seaton. The photographs which chronicle this fascinating story have been supplied by Edward Crawforth, John Meredith, Vic Mitchell, John Price, Terry Russell and Richard Wiseman. Extra photo-graphic help in preparing negatives for publication has been kindly given by Paul Swinney. Much information and archival material has been supplied by Mark Horner of the Seaton Tramway, and I am very indebted to him. I am also very grateful to David Howard, Managing Director of Eastbourne Buses for allowing me access to the departmental archives. Other valuable sources of information have been Allan Gardner, Roy Hubble and Stan Letts, all of whom have "notched up" many miles of service with the Seaton Tramway.

Although the emphasis in this volume is on historical photos, the Seaton Tramway is very much an up to date, go ahead concern which provides quality transport for local residents and holiday makers alike. All readers of this book, whether from home or abroad, are advised to make tracks to Seaton for a unique experience...they will not be disappointed.

GEOGRAPHICAL SETTING

Eastbourne is situated on the South Coast of England in the county of East Sussex. The tramway was located on relatively flat terrain separated from the beach by an area of shingle which stretched across the Crumbles to Langney Point.

The Devonshire seaside resort of Seaton is home to the present tramway which follows the old railway trackbed by the banks of the River Axe as far as Colyford. North of the level crossing with the A3052 the line rises through pleasant rolling countryside with meadows bordering the River Coly until the terminus is reached just outside the village of Colyton.

HISTORICAL
BACKGROUND

Claude W. Lane was a qualified electrical and mechanical engineer who ran the Lancaster Electrical Company from premises in Barnet, Hertfordshire. Battery electric delivery vehicles were the mainstay of production, but in 1949 there emerged from the works a remarkable miniature tramcar set to run on newly laid 15ins./381mm gauge tracks. The fame of car 23 spread and soon the owner had assembled portable track and overhead wires so that operation could be moved to various local fetes and garden parties. Thus it was that the passenger carrying, miniature tramway made its debut on 2nd June 1949 in the grounds of Hadley House, Barnet. A second tram, open boat car 225, joined the original car 23 in 1950. Both vehicles later appeared for the summer season on a short stretch of track at West Marina, St.Leonards, and this experience was the first stage in the search to find a permanent site for the tramway. Attention then switched to Voryd Park, Rhyl, North Wales where around a quarter of a mile of single track was constructed to accommodate the growing fleet which included four wheel, open top car 3, constructed in 1952. Although the line in North Wales was successful and operated from 1952 to 1957, expansion plans and the setting up of a new company - Modern Electric Tramways Ltd. - on 19th May 1953, resulted in the search for a more suitable permanent site. This was found on the South Coast of England just outside the popular seaside resort of Eastbourne.

Track laying at Eastbourne commenced in March 1954 and the gauge chosen was the wider 2ft./610mm which offered greater stability for the planned new batch of tramcars. The official opening of the line by the Mayor of Eastbourne occurred at Whitsun 1955 and paying customers had the opportunity to ride two new cars, one of which was a fully enclosed double deck tram, in fact a larger version of pioneer car 23. This vehicle, car 238, marked the end of the miniature era, as the next addition to the rolling stock was the more substantial car 6 which could cope with up to 40 passengers - in short a narrow gauge tramcar in its own right. Life then settled

down for Claude Lane and his associate, Allan Gardner; the popularity of the tramway was assured and improvements to track, overhead and buildings followed. However, the mid 1960s brought concerns over the long term plans of the local council who wanted to remove the tramway because it was in the way of a new feeder road system joining Langney to Royal Parade. In the face of these threats the management of the company looked elsewhere for a secure freehold site and negotiations began with British Railways to purchase the disused trackbed of the former Seaton branch line in Devon.

September 17th 1969 marked the end of tramway operation in Eastbourne and the massive task of transferring all the stock and equipment to Seaton began. This effort bore fruit in the inauguration of the first section of tramway on 27th August 1970. Since there was as yet no overhead wire, car 8 was hitched to a battery truck. The permanent way was constructed to a gauge of 2ft. 9ins./838mm.

This start was somewhat clouded by the sudden death on 2nd April 1971 of Claude Lane. However, Allan Gardner was on hand to assume the mantle of Managing Director and progress continued unabated. By the end of 1973 overhead wire had been erected along the whole length of track from Seaton Depot to Colyford. A pressing need for the company was to raise the profile of the trams by extending the line nearer to the centre of town. This was achieved by a new right of way from the depot to a terminus by the car park adjacent to Harbour Road. This extension was duly opened on 17th May 1975. Later in the same year the first steps were taken on the northern route to Colyton with the installation in November of the regauged level crossing at Colyford. The staff and volunteers then set to work on reballasting the track bed on the extension in readiness for the new permanent way. Problems were encountered with the elements which delayed construction and forced the company to adopt flood protection measures. On 8th March 1980 the task was complete and the full tramway was finally operational.

Increased passenger demands have since resulted in more trams appearing on the line and the company now looks forward to the Millenium with confidence. Truly much has been achieved over the span of fifty years and all those connected with the company can look back with pride on the progress from a temporary miniature line used for garden fetes to a full scale transport system.

A sales brochure from Claude Lane's company

THE EARLY LINES

1.   Claude Lane is seen on the platform of Blackpool standard car 99 in the 1940s. Tram driving was a seasonal occupation for him and the winter months were spent in planning and building his own tramway system! (Seaton Tramway)

2.   The big day arrives and car 23 is pictured on its public debut at Hadley House. The event is so popular that John Price, the photographer, is obliged to climb up a ladder to get a better view. By all accounts trade seems brisk on this July day in 1949. Note the temporary overhead wire which carried 60 volts dc to the car motors. (J.H.Price)

3.   The date is 1st August 1949 and the scene changes to Uxbridge Agricultural Show where a loop of track has been laid to accommodate car 23. As is usual in miniature attractions, the kids don't have it all their own way, and a rather overscale adult face peeps out from the lower deck…perhaps mum is looking after her youngster.   (J.H.Meredith)

4. On the sea front at St.Leonards car 23 is joined by boat car 225. This photo shows clearly the fifteen inch gauge track and the rather cramped conditions for any passenger who had already left primary school! Nevertheless the novelty of this occasion has attracted a crowd of grown ups all decked out in their best July 1951 fashions. (J.H.Meredith)

5. The crowds have departed leaving car 225 to convey the populus on this rather raw day in August 1951. The operation here only lasted one season, but electric traction could still be enjoyed on the other side of the main road in the shape of the Hastings and District trolleybuses. The local trams and trolleybuses are featured in two companion Middleton Press volumes. (J.H.Meredith)

6. The line at Rhyl stretched from Promenade, West Parade to Wellington Road Coach Park. Here car 3 is depicted on the single track. This tram was constructed in response to customer demands for a traditional British design to complement the other two more modern looking cars. (Rev.N.E.Lempriere)

7. We arrive at Eastbourne appropriately in time to catch sight of car 6, the first of the non-miniature trams. Here it stands at Princes Park terminus in the late 1950s.
(Seaton Tramway)

8. The fourteen year old novice motorman at the controls of car 2 is none other than the present author who was photographed on a visit to the tramway in August 1964. Above the tram a trolley reverser has now been added so that the pole does not have to be swung at the terminus. (R.J.Harley)

9. In the mid-1960s another track was laid for car 01 which saw service as a tram shop. It was in fact a rebuild of miniature car 226, and it emerged in this new state in 1965. At ground level next to car 01 we observe Messrs Lane and Gardner engaged in very necessary maintenance of the pointwork. (Seaton Tramway)

11. Car 238 is about to depart with a full load. The short upper deck platforms over the driver were a favourite spot for the author - not only was there a good view of the line ahead, but also no adult could fit up there to disturb the juvenile appreciation of the ride. (R.J.Harley Coll.)

10. An array of company motive power greets the visitor on 10th September 1966. In this animated scene a group of customers clusters round the tram shop whilst the gentleman on the right takes one more shot for the album. (J.H.Price)

12. Oh Dear! An embarrassing moment for J.W.Fowler, founding member of the Light Railway Transport League (later LRTA), as he splits the points in car 238. The presence of a number of camera equipped tramway fanatics recording the scene probably didn't help. However, a neat reversing movement will soon put matters right. (T.Russell)

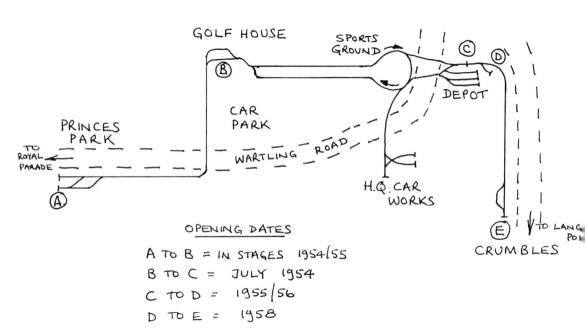

Diagram of the Eastbourne Tramway.

13. Before we leave the terminus we notice the new waiting shelter on the left of the picture. In the shelter during the summer months there was usually a display of postcard size views of various British systems; this served to whet the appetite of many a youthful enthusiast eager to investigate the nation's tramway heritage. (R.J.Harley Coll.)

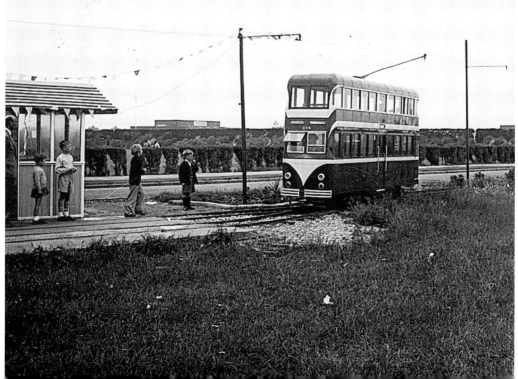

14. The passage of trams over the sharp bend by the car park crossing was normally accompanied by the squealing of wheel flanges as they bit into the curved rails. In this 1967 view more substantial traction standards have been erected. The long, flat building in the right hand background is the Modern Electric Tramways car works. (J.H.Price)

54. In 1974 car 12 took part in a six month experiment sponsored by Brecknell Willis, the manufacturers of the pantograph seen attached to the car roof. On termination of the trials normal trolley pole current collection was resumed. (J.H.Price)

55. Car 8 has just negotiated the loop parallel to the River Axe. The banks of the river are rich in bird life, amongst the species which may be observed from a passing tramcar are: curlews, oystercatchers, redshanks, herons, shelducks, teals, gulls, swans and even the odd kingfisher. (J.H.Price)

56. Battery operation is still the order of the day as this tram swings out of Swan's Nest Loop and heads towards Bobsworth Bridge. (J.H.Price)

57. November sunshine in 1976 warms Allan Gardner and David Chaplyn as they work on top of works car 02. They are connecting up the overhead running wire for the left hand track at Colyford. (S.E.Letts)

58. We reach the site of Colyford where a low platform is being built in this April 1973 view. The works car provides a convenient base and shelter for the construction crew. (Seaton Tramway)

59. Car 16 is on a test run in 1991 before its entry into service. Here it rests at Colyford. Note the NEXT TRAM platform indicator board and the sign directing patrons to the nearby hostelry of the White Hart. The Seaton Tramway has been instrumental in providing transport for many a thirsty traveller seeking a "swift half" before continuing his journey. (Seaton Tramway)

60. Another trial run, this time in September 1973, sees car 12 in its original single deck condition at Colyford. The narrow gauge tramway tracks end by the former railway level crossing and the northern extension to Colyton must wait until further funds and materials are available. (J.H.Price)

61. Colyford Station opened with Seaton branch line on 16th March 1868. It saw its last train on 7th March 1966. Just over ten years later car 7 represents the new regime as it waits for the return to Seaton. (J.H.Meredith)

62. The summer of 1976 was famous for the longest spell of dry weather in living memory. Here the sign leaves no doubt as to the transport awaiting the visitor to a parched Colyford which hadn't seen any rain for weeks. (S.E.Letts)

63. Trolley trouble by the level crossing holds up the progress of car 6; the trolley head is actually entangled in a cable used to supply power to the lighting. On this day absolutely no illumination is needed for the prominent warning sign for northbound tramcars! (R.Hubble)

64. At 11.30pm on 15th November 1975 work started on excavating the level crossing with the main road to replace the former standard gauge BR track with grooved tram rails laid to the Seaton gauge. Car 12 was positioned nearby to supply soup and other necessities for the work-force who laboured all night to complete the job by 8.00am the following morning. This picture shows car 2 whose right of way has been pro-tected by the standard Department of Transport flashing lights. (Seaton Tramway)

65. There are two loops between Colyford and Colyton Terminus. Car 12 moves aside to let the permanent way team pass at Tye Lane in August 1982. (R.Hubble)

66. The installation of the points at Tye Lane in April 78 is not helped by a cold wind which sweeps across a landscape still showing no signs of spring. (R.Hubble)

67. The weather has improved since the previous view and car 12 is again on hand to test the new alignment. Note that in this August 1979 photograph the extension is still only partially wired and the overhead is not in place right through from Colyford to Colyton. (R.Hubble)

68. This single track, electric tramway in a rural landscape conjures up visions of years past in Europe - the Belgian Vicinal in the Ardennes or the meandering lines of the Haute Vienne in the hills south of Limoges - however, this scene belongs to the present and the magic still survives here at the Riding School stop near Cownhayne Loop. (R.Hubble)

69. We enter the grounds of the former Colyton
Station and observe car 8 in Silver Jubilee livery
as it passes the old goods shed.
(A.J.V.Gardner)

70. A family gets a good view from the back of
car 17 as it leaves Colyton in June 1995. On the
left of the picture are the remains of the former
railway platform. (V.Mitchell)

71. On 10th June 1995 car 16 waits to depart for Seaton. Major construction work has since taken place at this location and the company has plans to repave and realign the track, whilst the remaining station buildings will be upgraded. (V.Mitchell)

→

72. After lying dormant for many years since the branch line closed in 1966, Colyton Station reopened for rail traffic on 8th March 1980. In this pleasant September 1990 scene car 14 is framed by trees and shrubs which add colour and enhance the atmosphere of the old station. (M.Horner)

→

73. On show at Colyton at the June 1995 Bus Rally was this quarter scale London Transport M class tramcar, built by Vic Mitchell and powered by a Sinclair C5 motor. The Middleton Press sales caravan was also in attendance. (V.Mitchell)

74. At the stub terminal car 8 stands before the trolley is swung and the top deck seats are reversed for the return journey. (E.Crawforth)

75. In August 1981 car 4 is caught on film performing the last departure of the day from Colyton. As the tram is about to make its way through the gathering dusk, the string of bright lights imparts a rather special quality to this summer's evening. (R.Hubble)

76. Much of the remaining trackbed of the old railway north of Colyton has reverted to farm land, therefore a further extension of the tramway is very unlikely. Here at the end of the line we note on the edge of the picture the Ruston class 48 diesel loco which was acquired in May 1973 to assist construction work. (R.J.S.Wiseman)

BUILDING AND MAINTAINING THE TRAMWAY

77. Mechanical help is enlisted at Poppy Corner, Seaton in March 1994. Because the line is a public carrier, great attention must be paid to all safety aspects which include the close monitoring of the permanent way and the renewal of the track bed pictured here. (M.Horner)

78. In the cutting approaching Colyton Station a set of rails has been deposited on the new ballast; these rails will later be properly aligned by the track gang. The onward march of traction poles may just be discerned in the distance. (S.E.Letts)

79. Colyford on 12th April 1973 and the track bed has been levelled in readiness for ballasting. On the right of the shot is that tribute to Victorian plumbing, a cast iron urinal, which has survived from London and South Western Railway days. (Seaton Tramway)

80. Essential track maintenance is in the capable hands of Fred Chubb as he fits a new fishplate at Tye Lane Loop in May 1980. (R.Hubble)

81. Work at Colyton is progressing in April 1978 with a variety of the company's service fleet on display. Overhead wires have yet to appear, therefore traction is supplied by the Ruston diesel pictured at the rear of works car 02. (R.Hubble)

82. Traction poles were bought from the Eastbourne Corporation Lighting Department. After de-rusting treatment they were all given three coats of specialist paint to guard against the salt laden winds which blow in from the English Channel. Poles are planted to a depth of three feet (914mm) in the ground and are then set in concrete. This picture is dated 23rd June 1973 and shows the traction standards ready to receive the overhead running wire. (J.H.Price)

83. Above Swan's Nest Loop repairs are made to the overhead before the next service tram can proceed into the loop. The Seaton overhead is energised at 120 volts dc. (R.Hubble)

84. A carbon insert from the trolley head is replaced. Apart from the short lived 1974 experiment with pantographs, the Seaton company has remained faithful to the traditional British trolley pole method of current collection. (R.Hubble)

85. The standard truck favoured by Seaton is based on the maximum traction design once used extensively in London. Here the truck of car 2 has been run out for inspection. The depot also has maintenance pits so that attention can be paid to the underside of each tramcar. Plans have since been prepared for an extension to the depot and an upgrade to facilities will include an all weather paint shop, a full length pit and extra office space. (R.Hubble)

86. The public image of the tramway is very important, therefore it is vital that the cars are well turned out and attractively painted. The careful work of giving car 14 that extra shine is observed within the confines of Riverside Depot. (R.Hubble)

87. Stan Letts is one of the several skilled volunteers who have enhanced the image of the tramway. The work of producing transfers and ornate lettering is a labour of love, and the finished product will add to the smart appearance of the fleet. (D. Voice)

88. The top device depicts a trolley wheel encircled by a simple buckled garter in green, bearing the company's original title. Underneath we see the red, oval buckled garter with the company's Seaton title in gold letters.
(S.E.Letts)

89. Car 23 was built in 1949 as an all enclosed, double deck tram. It was the first of the "miniature" trams and it was finally sold in 1958. Here it is seen at St.Leonards on 11th August 1951. Note the young lady sitting above the driver's cabin.   (J.H.Meredith)

90. Car 23 has now been preserved by an enthusiast from Merseyside and it paid a visit to Seaton on 15th July 1995 as part of the celebrations connected with the tramway's silver jubilee.   (M.Horner)

SEATON TRAMWAY
East Devon

6 MILE TRIP
THROUGH AXE AND COLY VALLEYS

BRITAINS ONLY
OPEN-TOP DOUBLE DECKER TRAMS
OPERATING ON 2'·9" GUAGE

IN DAILY SERVICE, APRIL-NOVEMBER
LIMITED WINTER SERVICE

PARTIES & INFORMATION ☎ 0297-21702
or write HARBOUR RD, SEATON, E. DEVON.

91. Car 3 stands outside the depot at Eastbourne on 21st August 1955. This vehicle is an accurate model of a traditional British, four wheel, open top tram. When company policy began to favour larger vehicles, it appeared less in service. (J.H.Meredith)

92. In this picture dated 16th September 1962 work is under way to add an open balcony, top deck to car 3. This was intended for display purposes only, but the conversion was halted when an American buyer put in an offer for car 3 in its original open top state. The tram was then sold. On the Seaton Tramway fully enclosed, double deck cars have been ruled out due to height restrictions and concerns about the comfort of passengers. (J.H.Price)

93. Car 238 was built in 1955 as a replica of a Blackpool eight wheel car. This miniature vehicle also rode on two equal wheel trucks. It was really a single deck car, however, a short canopy over each driver's cab contained seating for children. It was eventually sold with cars 3 and 225 (a miniature open boat tram) to America. (J.H.Meredith)

94. The chassis of former boat car 226 is seen here during conversion to shop car 01. This picture dates from the winter of 1964/5 and Claude Lane is standing on the car.
(Seaton Tramway)

95. At Eastbourne the mobile tram shop was an inspired idea which generated more revenue for the company. As the name board suggests there are all sorts of "goodies" inside to induce the enthusiast and the holiday maker to part with his cash. (R.J.Harley Coll.)

96. The tram shop metamorphosed at Seaton into an unpowered trailer car, it was also re-painted from its original bright red to an equally bright yellow and white livery. One of the features in the shop window used to be a large model of a London tram, which unfortunately was not for sale. (R.Hubble)

97. During a lull in the proceedings Jean Hubble is photographed inside the tram shop. The duties of the guardian of this particular car could be arduous especially on fine days when, as seen in picture 33, there was a rush for the tramway. The days of mobile tram shop car 01 are now over and the vehicle is at present stored pending conversion to the works fleet. (R. Hubble)

98. Car 4 was constructed in 1961. It is based on a well known design originating with Blackpool Corporation, and is seen in service at Eastbourne. It has a seating capacity of 20. (J.H. Price)

99. After its transfer to Seaton car 4 retained its Eastbourne livery of green and cream. It also retained its popularity and on fine days this tram offers a wonderfully invigorating ride along the Axe Valley. (V.Mitchell)

100. Works car 02 owes its origins to a vehicle ordered by the Air Ministry in 1954. It was first fitted, as depicted here, with a single truck, but now runs on bogies at Seaton. It received a new body in 1981.   (J.H.Meredith)

15. At Golf House the first passing loop was encountered. The tram stop sign was later replaced by an ex Llandudno and Colwyn Bay version. Car 6 is shown with its original toastrack lower deck. This was altered in 1962 to include two end saloons, but this arrangement failed to find favour and the toastrack was reinstated in 1990. (Seaton Tramway)

EASTBOURNE, CAR DEPOT
TO CRUMBLES TERMINUS

16. At the end of the 1964 season a Tramway Museum Society special was run using car 2. In this scene a tram load of aficionados passes on the opposite track to the Crumbles bound line which has been relaid in heavier girder rail. This track doubling was carried out in 1964 ; ex Blackpool and ex Sheffield grooved rail was employed. (J.H.Price)

17. Car 3 nears the depot on 4th July 1954. The couple sitting on the top deck seem somewhat overscale for this particular vehicle. (J.H.Price)

18. We look back in single track days towards the Golf House. The section from Golf House to the car depot was the first to open in July 1954. The approaching open car runs past the line of trees which once existed at this location. Nowadays there is no wind break and the Channel gales sweep across an unattractive expanse of highway. (T.Russell)

19. Outside the depot, Claude Lane attends to the mechanical needs of car 6 whilst car 238 passes en route to the Crumbles.
(Seaton Tramway)

→

20. Everyone has gone to lunch in this August 1964 scene. Car 7 waits in the sunshine after the motorman has retired to a nearby caravan to enjoy his midday break. In those days most of the visitors would have been on full board at a hotel or guest house and they would emerge again in the afternoon to resume their holiday.
(R.J.Harley)

→

21. The bus to the right of car 7 is a scaled down version of a London General B type. It was constructed by Claude Lane in 1956 using the chassis of a 1929 Swift. Its main duties were to patrol along Royal Parade through the town to Eastbourne Pier in order to advertise the tramway. The vehicle now resides at the back of Riverside Depot, Seaton in a dismantled state.
(Seaton Tramway)

EASTBOURNE TRAMWAYS

(Associated with Modern Electric Tramways Ltd.)

Princes Park, Eastbourne.

FARES

Royal Parade

to Golf House	-	-	-	2d.
„ Sports Ground	-	-	-	4d.
„ Boundary (Terminus)	-	-	-	6d.
Cheap Return	-	-	-	10d.

Infants in arms — Free.

Passengers with Return tickets may alight at the Terminus and return by a later Tram if they so wish.

TIMES

Daily Service (Including Sundays) 10 a.m. — 10 p.m.

LINE

Length of Line : 1 mile (with 5 passing loops).
Track Gauge : 2 feet.
Line Voltage : 72 volts D.C.

ROLLING STOCK

Six passenger carrying trams and one engineering car with two non-powered wagons.

CURRENT

The current is generated in the company's works by two Blackstone Oil Engines driving D.C. generators. The current is fed to the line from the main switchboard, and to two sub-stations, one at the Royal Parade and one at the Golf House where a supply is also taken from the Electricity Board.

GENERAL

This system is now the only Tramway in the country South of Sheffield, and the only Tramway in the world using double-deck cars on a two foot gauge line.

All the Trams are built and maintained by the company in their works. It is hoped in the near future to extend the line both eastwards and westwards.

22. Car 02 stands on the connecting track from the depot to the works in the background. At the time of the photo this vehicle had just been rebuilt in anticipation of the move to Seaton. (Seaton Tramway)

23. On 18th September 1960 another works tram is pictured in front of company HQ. This car's appearance definitely owes something to an American street railway, flat car. (J.H.Price)

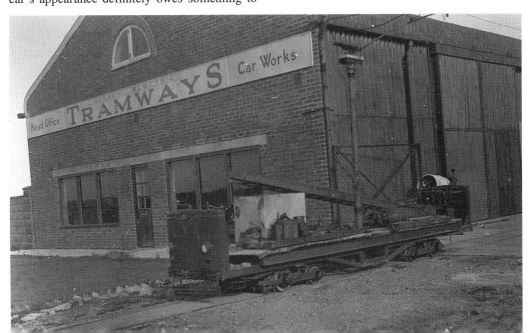

24. A peep inside the works reveals cars 2 and 4 stored out of service. Note that car 4 is positioned over an inspection pit. This head office cum works building was completed in October 1958 and was later demolished after the closure of the Eastbourne Tramway. (R.J.Harley)

25. Round the back of the depot was situated the original 1955 terminus of the tramway. A couple of redundant traction poles frame car 238 as it returns from the Crumbles extension which opened at Whitsun 1958.   (Seaton Tramway)

26. At the same spot as the last photo we observe a minor contretemps after the front bogie of the tram has parted company with the rails. There was a short stub siding behind the depot and in this case some "unauthorised person" has interfered with the points. One hopes Allan Gardner and his rescue crew will take the advice of the advertisement on the side of the car! (T.Russell)

27. The line from the depot to Crumbles Boundary was first laid in the winter of 1957/58, but due to a legal dispute it all had to be repositioned further south of the parallel road. Here car 02 pulls a hopper truck over the new alignment. (Seaton Tramway)

28. We finally arrive at the end of the track. In the distant haze is the line of the South Downs which end in spectacular cliffs by Beachy Head. In the foreground the vista has changed dramatically since this shot was taken in 1964. In 1996 a view from this location would show new highways and the large Sovereign Leisure Centre which now dominates the scene. (R.J.Harley)

Want a Change?

Then have a Ride across

The Crumbles

by . . .

TRAM

from

Princes Park Gate

The only Tramway in the World using
Double-Deck Cars on a 2ft. gauge

Daily Service (including Sundays) 10 a.m. - 10 p.m.

Fares: **Royal Parade**
to **Golf House**	- -	**2d.**
„ **Sports Ground** -	-	**4d.**
„ **Boundary (Terminus)**		**6d.**
Cheap Return	- -	**10d.**

**Princes Park is at the Eastern End of Promenade
and reached by Blue Bus Nos. 6, 6a & 8**

Christian the Printer, Eastbourne

29. Claude Lane swings the pole and most passengers have already flipped over their seats for the return journey. The rails actually ended a few yards short of the then borough boundary. It seems the local council which ran its own motor buses (described fully in *Eastbourne Bus Story* - Middleton Press album) feared that if the tracks crossed the boundary, then the tramway company would have been in a position to sell its operation and running rights to the rival Southdown Motor Services. (J.H.Meredith)

Other views appear in *Eastbourne to Hastings* in the Middleton Press South Coast Railways series.

SEATON TERMINUS TO
SEATON DEPOT

30. Our first encounter with the Seaton Tramway takes place at the splendid new town terminus officially opened on 26th August 1995. The architecture of the ticket office and waiting shelter blends sympathetically with car 17 as it prepares to depart for the journey to Colyton. (Seaton Tramway)

31. On 10th June 1995, a few weeks before the opening, we note the tracks in the foreground which lead to the new terminus. Meanwhile car 4 has arrived at the old terminal loop and the motorman hauls on the trolley rope which boasts the Red Ensign. (V.Mitchell)

32. The photographer has now moved behind car 4 and we observe final preparations in advance of the installation of overhead wires at the new terminus. This was an evening run on the occasion of the annual Bus Rally. (V.Mitchell)

33. The date is 24th August 1976 and the popularity of the trams is very evident. On this day four cars are maintaining a 12 minute service from 10.30am to 9.30pm, with a break for lunch from 12.30pm to 2.30pm. Conductors are positioned at each end of the cars and they are issuing tickets for an adult return fare of 35p, with a 25p reduced rate for a child.
(J.H.Meredith)

34. We move in closer with the crowds as car 2 loads for an imminent get away. Car 6 waits its turn to be boarded. (J.H.Meredith)

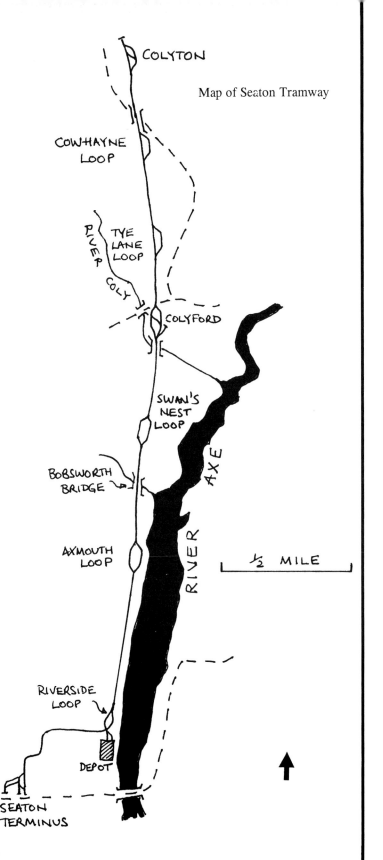

Map of Seaton Tramway

COLYTON

COWHAYNE
LOOP

RIVER COLY

TYE
LANE
LOOP

COLYFORD

SWAN'S
NEST
LOOP

BOBSWORTH
BRIDGE

RIVER AXE

AXMOUTH
LOOP

½ MILE

RIVERSIDE
LOOP

DEPOT

SEATON
TERMINUS

35. Swing that pole! This is
the first of two views taken
in contrasting seasons. First
we observe motorman Roy
Hubble doing the honours in
the snow on a dull January
day in 1985. (R.Hubble)

36. Open bench car 17 her-
alds the arrival of Spring and
up pops Stan Letts, who is
taking a break from his other
duties in order to help out
with the driving. The gentleman glimpsed on the ex-
treme right of the picture is
one of the many foreign visitors to the line. He has come
all the way from California
to experience the unique
Seaton atmosphere.
(S.E.Letts)

37. On safari in September 1985 and car 8 encounters a Lioness in the car park. In the driving seat of the old Leyland is the well known, West Country bus preservationist, Colin Shears. (S.E.Letts)

38. We now watch car 14 leaving the terminus; this tram is rostered on a short working to Colyford only. In the background car 17 is on hand to cater for passenger late arrivals. (E.Crawforth)

39. Slowly does it, as car 8 edges round the last curve before the car park. The warning sign hanging from the overhead does not encourage any Grand Prix performances on this bend! Two miles per hour is the order of the day in this April 1980 view. (R.J.S.Wiseman)

40. Its an enthusiasts' day out as we approach the depot on 10th June 1995, when a vintage bus rally swells the numbers of tram riders. (E.Crawforth)

←———

41. We are present at the September 1973 fleet review in front of the depot. The leading tram has its trolley pole connected by a cable to a battery truck. This supplied power in the absence of overhead wires outside the depot area. Note the partially completed curve in the right foreground; this is the first stage of the extension from the depot to the car park.   (J.H.Price)

42. It is 20th June 1971 and the River Axe can be seen to the left of the depot. Tracklaying has begun in earnest and in the next few months much time and effort will be required from volunteers and staff to complete the route to Colyford. In the meantime car 2 waits to perform the shuttle service up the line to Bobsworth Bridge, so named because the fare was one shilling (5p) - a "bob" in old parlance. (J.H.Price)

43. Car 2 is hitched up to the battery truck whilst the depot doors open to admit a party of enthusiasts. (J.H.Price)

44. Cars 12, 17 and 2 are seemingly imprisoned in this August 1989 shot of Riverside Depot. (M.Horner)

45.   Like Thomas Gray's ploughman who "homeward plods his weary way", the last car of the day rolls in as the shadows lengthen. The beautiful wooded slopes of the Axe Valley basking in the evening sunshine serve to inspire a modern elegy of rural tranquility. (M.Horner)

46.   Inside the depot there is the usual treasure trove of objects to fascinate the tramway buff. Here cars 12 and 14 are seen in August 1975. The latter car is in the process of being rebuilt from former Metropolitan Electric Tramways car 94, constructed in 1904. (R.Hubble)

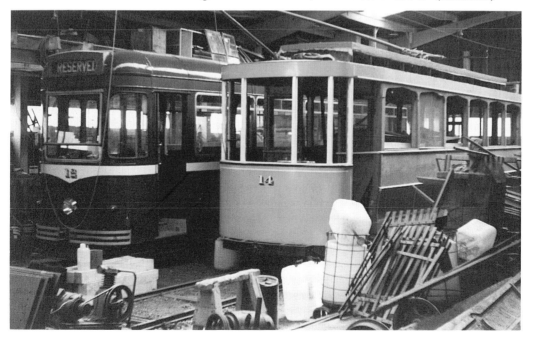

47. We catch a glimpse of the open top bus parked behind car 4. The tram is fitted with ex Glasgow seats and possesses sundry other electrical equipment from the former Llandudno and Colwyn Bay line. (J.H.Price)

48. In true prototype fashion the top deck railings of car 7 have been suspended from the depot roof pending renovation of the lower half of the tram. Similar photographs of repair work on another narrow gauge tramway can be viewed in companion album *Thanet's Tramways*. (R.Hubble)

49. In addition to maintaining the present fleet, future projects include the restoration of this former Exeter tramcar. The intention is to place it on a three axle truck, which will be a novelty as far as British tramways are concerned. (E.Crawforth)

RIVERSIDE LOOP TO COLYFORD

50. The 1981 summer season caught up with the company before it could finish the refurbishment of car 8. In this October scene the tram will have run all season clad in just primer and undercoat (the advertisements had been paid for and the tram had to run). At Riverside Loop it meets car 14 which has just been mounted on its trucks for its first trial spin up the line. (S.E.Letts)

51. Trams pass on the right at Riverside Loop contrary to the usual British left handed rule of the road. Car 8 is pictured opposite car 16 which is obscuring car 6. All trams are timed at three minutes between loops and four minutes from Riverside to Seaton Terminus. Signals are not employed to control single track sections, but a staff token is used to protect the depot to car park route. (Seaton Tramway)

PASS

177

M..

ON ALL ELECTRIC TRAMCARS AT

EASTBOURNE.

Valid until..

DATE OF ISSUE

For MODERN ELECTRIC TRAMWAYS LTD.
ENGINEER & MANAGER.

IMPORTANT—To be returned immediately on expiry.
NOT TRANSFERABLE.

52. On the straight track from Riverside Loop to Axmouth Loop a line of unfinished traction poles retreats into the distance. The date is 16th July 1972 and the overhead wiring has yet to be installed. (J.H.Price)

53. This is the same date as the previous photo,
but we are now looking in the opposite direction
as car 8 coasts towards the depot. (J.H.Price)

101. This June 1995 view shows the current state of car 02. The enlarged, roof mounted, inspection platform allows much needed space for many important overhead maintenance jobs. (E.Crawforth)

102. Constructed in 1958 car 7, like sister vehicle car 6, is based on the double truck, open top trams which once plied between Llandudno and Colwyn Bay. Indeed, the top deck seats come from one of the ex Bournemouth cars which worked on the LCBER in North Wales. (Seaton Tramway)

SEATON TRAMWAY
SILVER JUBILEE

The Directors request the presence of

_____

to the Official Opening of the New Terminus
at Harbour Road Car Park
on Saturday August 26th 1995
Buffet Lunch - from 12 noon, at Seaton Youth Centre
followed by the Official Opening at 2.30 p.m.

Please Tear Off and Return this slip to the address below _____

R.S.V.P. by 1.8.1995 to Riverside Depot, Harbour Road, Seaton

103. Car 8 has seats for 43 passengers and after undergoing trials in Eastbourne in 1969, it first entered revenue service at Seaton. Since this view was taken in 1976, the tram has been rebodied so that the lower deck is now divided into a number of transverse, toast rack seats. (J.H.Meredith)

104. Eastbourne works out-shopped car 2 in 1963/4. It is painted in bright red, it seats 35 and possesses two "Robinson" type split staircases. In this early Seaton scene it is depicted coupled to a battery truck. (R.J.Harley Coll.)

SEATON TRAMWAY — **Excess Fare Ticket**

Issued by Travelling Ticket Staff

SEATON

Tram ——————— Date ———————
(month in words)

Ticket held No. ——————— Description ———————

To ——————— From ———————

Via ———————

Excessed to ———————

From ———————

Via ———————

Cause & Description of Excess	Class	No. of Passengers (in words)		Amount £	
		Single	Return		
Adults without tickets					
Short of Destination					
Out of Date					
Difference Between					
Children Without Tickets					

Valid until ——————— Collected by ———————
* Not Transferable

105. Car 2 appears in this 1995 view and is little altered from its original condition; the only minor changes visible are the newer paint scheme and the larger, more ornate fleet numeral. (V.Mitchell)

106. A radical departure from the "traditional" Eastbourne fleet was marked by the construction of car 12 in 1965/6. This tram was built with winter operation in mind and it seated 20 people in an all enclosed saloon. In this picture we observe the partially completed car.
(Seaton Tramway)

107. In the author's opinion this tram was the most handsome vehicle in the fleet. It was 31ft. 6ins./9.6 metres in length and 4ft. 10ins./ 1473mm wide. Livery was green and cream.
(J.H.Price)

108. As has been mentioned earlier, this vehicle was equipped in 1974 with an experimental pantograph. A similar Brecknell Willis current collector was also fitted to car 4. Both pantographs proved successful, although (as seen here) they were extended sideways to cope with some of the overhead which was positioned off centre of the track. (J.H.Price)

109. Conversion of car 12 to an open topper followed in 1978-80 and the seating capacity was thereby increased to 50 passengers.
(Seaton Tramway)

110. The revised version of car 12 waits at the car park in July 1983. The opportunity has been taken to dispense with the usual open top trolley standard and the trolley base is now positioned above the passengers on the upper deck. (J.H.Price)

111. Car 14 entered service in 1984, although the fabric of the vehicle dates back to MET car 94, built in 1904. At Seaton the lower deck was rebuilt to a narrower configuration and the car now seats 26. (R.Hubble)

112. As we position ourselves behind the trolley standard on the top deck of car 6, we notice the wooden slatted seats which are equipped with "keep dry" flaps in case of inclement weather. The white painted guard railings can always be used by top deck travellers as a convenient arm rest. (R.J.Harley)

113. The interior of car 16 looks very inviting with its elegant light fittings and comfortable, upholstered seats. Note the stylish clerestory top lights and the decorated ceiling panels.
(Seaton Tramway)

114. Some of the mysteries of tramcar building are disclosed in this view of car 16 at Riverside Depot. This vehicle is ex Bournemouth car 106 and is pictured in its original state in the Tramway Classics volume *Bournemouth and Poole Tramways*. There is still much work to do in replacing side panels, installing new dashes and inserting yards of new electrical cabling.
(M.Horner)

115. Exeter Corporation Tramways car 19 arrives at Seaton in September 1994. It is destined to become Seaton car 19, an enclosed single deck vehicle which will be mounted on a six wheel truck. There are several views of Exeter car 19 in Middleton Press album *Exeter and Taunton Tramways*. (M.Horner)

FESTIVITIES

116. This group photo was taken at Colyford on 23rd September 1973. The occasion was the first car to run on overhead power as far as the then northern terminus of the line.   (J.H.Price)

117. H.M. Queen Elizabeth's silver jubilee celebrations in 1977 saw many trams appropriately adorned with patriotic bunting. Here in August of that year car 4 is pictured with driver Mike Skeggs.   (R.Hubble)

118. Visits to the line have also been made by several media celebrities. On the inaugural run of car 14 in June 1984 Larry Grayson performed the honours. (R.Hubble)

119. Car 8 has been decorated with flags in August 1985 to mark the tramway's first fifteen years at Seaton.   (R.Hubble)

120. Allan Gardner stands proudly next to car 8 on its launch for the 1995 season which coincided with the Seaton Tramway's silver jubilee. This was a time of celebration for past achievements and the company now looks forward with confidence to the future.   (A.J.V.Gardner)

**Photographs of the railway
between Colyton and Seaton
appear in *Branch Lines to Seaton
and Sidmouth* - Middleton Press**

MP Middleton Press

Easebourne Lane, Midhurst. West Sussex. GU29 9AZ   Tel: 01730 813169 Fax: 01730 812601

. . . . . Write or telephone for our latest list . . . . .

BRANCH LINES
Branch Line to Allhallows
Branch Lines to Alton
Branch Lines around Ascot
Branch Line to Bude
Branch Lines around Canterbury
Branch Lines to East Grinstead
Branch Lines around Effingham Jn
Branch Lines to Exmouth
Branch Line to Fairford
Branch Line to Hawkhurst
Branch Lines to Horsham
Branch Lines to Ilfracombe
Branch Line to Lyme Regis
Branch Line to Lynton
Branch Lines around March
Branch Lines around Midhurst
Branch Line to Minehead
Branch Lines to Newport
Branch Line to Padstow
Branch Lines around Portmadoc 1923-46
Branch Lines around Porthmadog 1954-94
Branch Lines to Seaton & Sidmouth
Branch Line to Selsey
Branch Lines around Sheerness
Branch Line to Southwold
Branch Line to Swanage
Branch Line to Tenterden
Branch Lines to Torrington
Branch Lines to Tunbridge Wells
Branch Line to Upwell
Branch Lines around Weymouth

LONDON SUBURBAN RAILWAYS
Caterham and Tattenham Corner
Clapham Jn. to Beckenham Jn.
Crystal Palace and Catford Loop
Holborn Viaduct to Lewisham
London Bridge to Addiscombe
Mitcham Junction Lines
South London Line
West Croydon to Epsom
Willesden Junction to Richmond
Wimbledon to Epsom

STEAMING THROUGH
Steaming through Cornwall
Steaming through East Sussex
Steaming through the Isle of Wight
Steaming through Surrey
Steaming through West Hants
Steaming through West Sussex

GREAT RAILWAY ERAS
Ashford from Steam to Eurostar
Festiniog in the Fifties

COUNTRY BOOKS
Brickmaking in Sussex
East Grinstead Then and Now

SOUTH COAST RAILWAYS
Ashford to Dover
Bournemouth to Weymouth
Brighton to Eastbourne
Brighton to Worthing
Chichester to Portsmouth
Dover to Ramsgate
Hastings to Ashford
Ryde to Ventnor
Worthing to Chichester

SOUTHERN MAIN LINES
Bromley South to Rochester
Charing Cross to Orpington
Crawley to Littlehampton
Dartford to Sittingbourne
East Croydon to Three Bridges
Epsom to Horsham
Exeter to Barnstaple
Exeter to Tavistock
Faversham to Dover
Haywards Heath to Seaford
London Bridge to East Croydon
Orpington to Tonbridge
Sittingbourne to Ramsgate
Swanley to Ashford
Three Bridges to Brighton
Tonbridge to Hastings
Victoria to Bromley South
Waterloo to Windsor
Woking to Southampton
Yeovil to Exeter

COUNTRY RAILWAY ROUTES
Andover to Southampton
Bath to Evercreech Junction
Bournemouth to Evercreech Jn
Burnham to Evercreech Junction
Croydon to East Grinstead
East Kent Light Railway
Fareham to Salisbury
Guildford to Redhill
Porthmadog to Blaenau
Reading to Basingstoke
Reading to Guildford
Redhill to Ashford
Salisbury to Westbury
Strood to Paddock Wood
Taunton to Barnstaple
Westbury to Bath
Woking to Alton

TROLLEYBUS CLASSICS
Croydon's Trolleybuses
Woolwich & Dartford Trolleybuses

TRAMWAY CLASSICS
Aldgate & Stepney Tramways
Bournemouth & Poole Tramways
Brighton's Tramways
Bristol's Tramways
Camberwell & W. Norwood Tramways
Croydon's Tramways
Dover's Tramways
East Ham & West Ham Tramways
Eltham & Woolwich Tramways
Embankment & Waterloo Tramways
Exeter & Taunton Tramways
Greenwich & Dartford Tramways
Hampstead & Highgate Tramways
Hastings Tramways
Ilford & Barking Tramways
Kingston & Wimbledon Tramways
Lewisham & Catford Tramways
Maidstone & Chatham Tramways
North Kent Tramways
Portsmouth's Tramways
Southampton Tramways
Southend-on-sea Tramways
Thanet's Tramways
Victoria & Lambeth Tramways
Walthamstow & Leyton Tramways
Wandsworth & Battersea Tramways

OTHER RAILWAY BOOKS
Garraway Father & Son
Industrial Railways of the South East
London Chatham & Dover Railway
South Eastern Railway
War on the Line

MILITARY BOOKS
Battle over Portsmouth
Battle Over Sussex 1940
Blitz Over Sussex 1941-42
Bognor at War
Bombers over Sussex 1943-45
Military Defence of West Sussex

WATERWAY ALBUMS
Hampshire Waterways
Kent and East Sussex Waterways
London to Portsmouth Waterway
West Sussex Waterways

BUS BOOK
Eastbourne Bus Story

SOUTHERN RAILWAY ● VIDEOS ●
Memories of the Hayling Island Branc
Memories of the Lyme Regis Branch
War on the Line